T0380679

Relentless

By: Briley McPherson

WestBow
PRESS®
A DIVISION OF THOMAS NELSON
& ZONDERVAN

WestBow Press books may be ordered through booksellers or by contacting:

WestBow Press
A Division of Thomas Nelson & Zondervan
1663 Liberty Drive
Bloomington, IN 47403
www.westbowpress.com
844-714-3454

Scripture taken from the New King James Version® Copyright © 1982 by Thomas Nelson. Used by permission. All rights reserved.

ISBN: 979-8-3850-2893-1 (sc)
ISBN: 979-8-3850-2894-8 (e)

Library of Congress Control Number: 2024913699

Print information available on the last page.

WestBow Press rev. date: 7/30/2024

CONTENTS

Intro

I hope you enjoy this journal and I pray it benefits you in some way.

Disclaimer:
I am no mom expert by any means!
I am just simply sharing my opinion and experiences with you.

Dedication

I am dedicating this journal to my mom, there are no words and not enough space for all I could say, the main thing is……

Thank you mama

"Strength and dignity are her clothing, And she smiles at the future." Proverbs 31:25

Credits

Bible Verses- NASB1995 BIBLE

Color Scheme- My two beautiful daughters
Motherly Advice or Words from a Mama:

Debby Holland
Phyliss Henry
Angie Pedigo
Maggie Braswell
Lisa Gentry

Why the name Relentless?

When I think of one word I can describe a mother as is, relentless. A mother is relentless at loving her child. A mother is relentless at caring for her child. And a mother is relentless at protecting her child.

Proverbs 22:6
"Start child off on the way they
should go, and even when they are
old they will not turn from it."

Affirmations

Fill yourself up with great affirmations everyday. A good way to find yourself some affirmations is in the good book. Especially in the book of Proverbs.

Read Proverbs 31

On the two pages, write affirmations from Proverbs 31 that you see in yourself.

YES IT IS OKAY TO TALK
HIGHLY OF YOURSELF!!

Affirmations

_____

_____

_____

_____

_____

_____

_____

Affirmations

_____

_____

_____

_____

_____

_____

"I don't have time for all of that"

This phrase above is probably something everyone has heard
from someone in your life at one time or another.
It could have been said about something you were doing that they
didn't particularly think was necessary, important, or worth the time.

My point is this, God created us all different. Just because I like to go
metal detecting and you like to make sour dough bread, does not mean
either is more important than the other.

Or maybe, you like to spend more time cleaning and organizing
your house and others like to clean and organize their flowerbeds.

VERSES TO READ

Genesis 1:27	Matthew 10:30
Psalms 139:13	Jeremiah 1:5

Girl I gotta work on 9 outta 9 of these! What about you?

"But the fruit of the Spirit is love, joy, peace, patience, kindness, goodness, faithfulness, gentleness, self-control; against such things there is no law." Galatians 5:22-23

Galatians 5:22-23

_____

_____

_____

_____

_____

_____

_____

Advice from one mother to another....

Prayer: Help me give my children good roots, God.

"We want our plants to have roots that go deep, gripping rich soil, where they can grow sturdy and beautiful. As a mother, I pray that we furnish the kind of soil that develops deep, sturdy roots toward God, so our children will never deviate too far from their own beginning."

"I have no greater joy than to hear that my
children are walking in the truth."
3 John 1:4

-Debby Holland

Pray for your child/ children today

_____

_____

_____

_____

_____

_____

_____

_____

"Marigolds"

One plan to keep bugs away from my house in the spring
and summer is going to be marigolds. They are suppose
to be good at battling them pesky ole bugs away.

When I think of marigolds in a spiritual sense, I think of sisters in
Christ. Ones who will pray for you in a time of battle in your life.

Whether you are going through mental, emotional, physical stress or
pain. Having those sisters in your life can help you with your battles.

Read Daniel 2:17-18

Luke 10:38-42

READ THE VERSES ABOVE........

Yeah, I bet some of you is like me, thinking we gotta have everything a certain way. The house needs to be picked up all the the time. All the dishes need to be done. I mean especially the laundry because when the basket is empty it ain't gonna get filled back up. WRONG LOL!

I think Jesus gave us women a very good example that we worry about many things. But, it is not all that important that I want my throw pillows and blankets off of the floor so I can sit down and not be anxious about that, haha. We need to choose that "what is better part" more often than things that are not so important.

*Have you been wanting to lay something at
God's feet that has been worrying you?
Use the next two journaling pages to talk with
HIM about your worrying........*

Lay your worries
at HIS feet

_____

_____

_____

_____

_____

_____

_____

Lay your worries
at HIS feet

_____

_____

_____

_____

_____

_____

_____

You are a voice!

Read Romans 12:10

If you see a mama struggling, encourage her, don't judge her. Who knows what kind of morning, day, or evening she has had.

Maybe saying "your a good mama" or "you got this mama" is what she might need in that very moment.

Sometimes, that is all us mothers need to hear.

Use the next page to journal about this verse

Romans 12:10

_____

_____

_____

_____

_____

_____

_____

"Angels among us"

One of the best pieces of advice I have ever received is from one of my best friends. She told me I had to give my kids to God. I mean completely give my kids to him. I would like to leave them at his feet and then go back in about 15 mins and pick them back up. Haha, it took me a long time to realize having them in HIS hands is WAY better than having them in mine. One verse that truly helped me understand how much more HE loves them than I do is in the book of Matthew.

READ
Matthew 18:10
*On the next page,
journal about what
you just read.*

Yeah girl, you read that right, your children
have their own personal angel......

_____

_____

_____

_____

_____

_____

Advice from one mother to another....

"First and foremost, keep your children in
your daily prayers regardless of their age.
Give them your undivided attention and
treasure the little things along the way.
Love them as God loves his children......
UNCONDITIONALLY!"

-Phyliss Henry

Read Mark 5:21-43

There are so many things we can pick up from these verses. Can you remember the day your child was born? That feeling never leaves you. When I read about this little girl's father in these scriptures and the faith he had in Jesus to help his little girl, it's truly humbling. I can not imagine th r fear and panic he was in for his little girl all while having the faith that Jesus could help her. In the meantime, headed to his house, they are stopped by a woman who has bleed for 12 years. This woman with the same faith just touches HIS cloak and she is healed. She done gone and tried to use all the magicians and they couldn't help her BUT JESUS' CLOAK healed THIS WOMAN. After this moving scene she pours out her heart to Jesus in front of a crowd of people and HE makes her WHOLE! She had so much faith to know something was going to happen. Now the little girl's daddy is like CMON JESUS!!! Can you imagine being her daddy? I would have been wanting to drag Jesus by the ear to get him to my baby! Haha. But, Jesus already knew he did not have to be in a hurry to get to the little girl. He knew what awaited at their home. Jesus says "ARISE" She wakes up! Can you imagine being her parents? Can you imagine the faith increase with your walk with Christ?

Take the next two pages and journal about these verses.

Mark 5: 21-43

_____

_____

_____

_____

_____

_____

_____

Mark 5: 21-43

_____

_____

_____

_____

_____

_____

_____

Laundry

I want to encourage you to thank
God for your laundry.
You might have 12 baskets full of laundry
right now, thank him for them. I know you're
thinking right now "Briley you have lost
your marbles", haha. I know, but somewhere
there is someone who CRAVES to have 12
baskets of laundry to do for their family.
Read Psalms 34:18

"A time"

Read ECCLESIASTES 3:11

We know HIS time is always best.
Take the next page to journal about
how this verse spoke to you.

Ecclesiastes 3:11

_____

_____

_____

_____

_____

_____

_____

Advice from one mother to another....

"Coach your kids. Don't just tell
then what to do and not to do.
Explain things to them using teachable
moments for right and wrong, good and bad,
healthy and unhealthy. Invest more time in
them than in electronic devices for yourself
or for them so as to build their character."

-Angie Pedigo

It is okay to ask for help

We all have those days where it is "all
over you" as my mom would say.
What she is meaning is you got a lot weighting
on you. You might just need 15 minutes to gather
yourself. Don't be too prideful to ask someone to
watch your kids so you can have that 15 minutes.
Read Matthew 11:28

Say a prayer for your mental and physical health today

_____

_____

_____

_____

_____

_____

_____

_____

"They don't come with a manual"

How many times have you ever heard this saying?
IT IS SO TRUE!!!!
We are not provided a manual to raise our precious children. The closest
thing I believe we have is God's word. And, we have a very incredible
woman to learn from in the Bible too, Mary, mother of Jesus.
Now take a few minutes and journal on the next couple of
pages of certain things about Mary that jumped out to you as
a mother. Remember, this is not about comparing yourself to
Mary. It is simply to help you learn how Mary showed so many
fruits of the spirit that she applied to her everyday life.

READ THESE VERSES

John 19: 25-30   Matthew 12: 46-50
John 2: 1-12   Luke 2: 41-52

John 19:25-30

_____

_____

_____

_____

_____

_____

_____

Matthew 12: 46-50

_____

_____

_____

_____

_____

_____

John 2: 1-12

_____

_____

_____

_____

_____

_____

_____

Luke 2: 41-52

_____

_____

_____

_____

_____

_____

_____

It is okay for you to have "me time"

This does not include grocery shopping or sitting on the toilet.

I heard a mama say one time……

"I used to not have to worry about me, but now I have to really take care of me so I can be the best of me for my kids."
-Maggie Braswell

On the next page, I want you to write down 3 things you can do for yourself to have "me time".

"Me time"

1 _____

2 _____

3 _____

What can I learn from these verses?

"But Jesus said, "Let the children alone, and do not hinder them from coming to Me; for the kingdom of heaven belongs to such as these."
Matthew 19:14

Matthew 19:14

_____

_____

_____

_____

_____

_____

A Friend

In my NKJV Bible the header of this start of these verses read "The Value of a Friend"

Read Ecclesiastes 4:9-10

I am sure we all have those 1-3 friends that we can always count on. I want to encourage you to reach out to those friends right now and just express how thankful you are God put them in your life.

On the next page, write down one of your favorite memories with one of your friends

Favorite memory
with friend

_____

_____

_____

_____

_____

_____

You Are Heard

READ HEBREWS 12:1-3

Sometimes mother's just need a listening ear!
That ear can be your friend Jesus.
Talk to him and have a raw conversation
about what might be on your heart.

Is there something that is just worrying you to pieces?

Is there something you are stressed about?

Is there a fear that you are ready to let go of?

**Take the next two journaling pages
to talk with your friend, Jesus**

"have a little talk with Jesus"

_____

_____

_____

_____

_____

_____

_____

"have a little talk with Jesus"

_____

_____

_____

_____

_____

_____

What does this verse mean to you?

"Every good thing given and every perfect gift is from above, coming down from the Father of lights, with whom there is no variation or shifting shadow."
James 1:17

James 1:17

_____

_____

_____

_____

_____

_____

_____

"Johnny"

My youngest daughter has a pony named, you guessed it, Johnny. Typically, my husband will lead her on her pony behind him on his horse. I got the opportunity to be the one to lead her on one ride. Little did I know my daughter has already picked up that if you kick your horse that it makes them go faster. As I was leading her, she would be back there just a kicking and her and Johnny would start to take off. I would have to make them stop because I had the control of his halter. I got to thinking to myself, how many times is God like my daughter, back there kicking and ready to go and I am pulling back because of fear, doubt, anxiety, etc.

READ VERSES

Psalms 34:4   Mark 11:23   Psalms 94:19

"Field Trip"

Ever now and then 2 of our 5 dogs like to go on a "field trip" as I like to call it. My old coonhound and my oldest daughter's dog like to roam around the woods for long periods of time. We have no clue where they venture off too and we never know when they are gonna show back up BUT they always do. They might show up on the back porch, they might show up on the front porch, or they might just come outta the woods somewhere on our property.

It makes me think of when I am praying for God to help me with something and I just can't figure out how HE is gonna make it happen or make it work.

BUT……. HE ALWAYS SHOWS UP!

READ JOHN 16:33

TAKE THE NEXT PAGE TO JOURNAL ABOUT THIS VERSE

John 16:33

_____

_____

_____

_____

_____

_____

"Paper towel"

One thing I did not realize when becoming a mother is that I would be a paper towel. My kids are all the time randomly just wiping things on me. It might be a booger, snot, cheeto hands, ice cream, or just basically anything they don't want on their hands.

I am really starting to wish I was more like this about things that bring me anxiety. I want to be better about just "wiping" it all on God. That's what HE wants me to do!

READ 1 PETER 5:7

USE THE NEXT PAGE TO JOURNAL ABOUT THIS VERSE
"WIPE" Your anxiety on him!

1 Peter 5:7

_____

_____

_____

_____

_____

_____

_____

How does this verse speak to you?

"Behold, children are a gift of the Lord,
The fruit of the womb is a reward."
Psalms 127:3

Psalms 127:3

_____

_____

_____

_____

_____

_____

_____

Advice from one mother to another....

"Consistency is an absolute must!!!
Without it, children are so confused and unsure of their place.
Never be afraid to admit to your child when you have made
a mistake and apologize to them and ask their forgiveness. I
learned what unconditional forgiveness truly is from my son,
whom I had to apologize to a lot. He forgave me every time.
Remember that our children belonged to God before they were ours.
He is able to protect and guard our children much better than we can.
Cover them in prayer always - morning, noon and night and
all times in between. Too much prayer never hurt anyone.
Love God, love your spouse, love your children.
In that order."

-Lisa Gentry

Advice from one mother to another….

*What is your motherly advice you
would give to someone?
Share on the next journal page*

Your Motherly Advice

_____

_____

_____

_____

_____

_____

Thank You!

I appreciate you reading this journal,
May God bless you and your family.

**"But I would feed you with the finest of the wheat, And
with honey from the rock I would satisfy you."
Psalms 81:16**

Printed in the United States
by Baker & Taylor Publisher Services